Language Lessons *for* Children

by Kathy Weitz

Primer Two Autumn
Student Book

Acknowledgements

Although my name is on the cover, the Primer series in many ways has been a collaborative effort. I owe a great debt of gratitude to many folks. The gorgeous cover designs are the craftsmanship of my friend Jayme Metzgar, with image credit to The Graphics Fairy (www.thegraphicsfairy.com). Many other friends have helped with both editing and content: in particular, Kimberlynn Curles, Emily Cook, Cheryl Turner, Karen Gill, Carolyn Vance, Lene Jaqua and the exceptional teachers, moms, and students of Providence Preparatory Academy. And of course, the main source of help and encouragement in myriad ways—from design consultation to field testing to dinner duty—has come from my dear husband and my wonderful children.

~kpw

© Copyright 2014. Kathy Weitz
Cottage Press
www.cottagepress.net

Printed in the United States of America.

All rights reserved. This book or any portion thereof may not be reproduced or used in any manner whatsoever without the express written permission of the publisher except for the use of brief quotations in a book review.

Primer Two Autumn
CONTENTS

Materials Needed for Primer Two Autumn vi

Week 1 3

The Land of Story-Books

Plurals
Writing Sentences
Days of the Week & Abbreviations
Rhyming Words

Week 2 13

from Early Days In Egypt

Past Tense
Homonyms
Synonyms
Plurals

Week 3 23

from Psalm 27

The Noun
Spelling Rule: **i** *Before* **e**
Rhyming Words
Antonyms
Homonyms & Synonyms
Past Tense & Plural

Week 4 33

from The Real Princess

Singular & Plural Nouns
Synonyms & Antonyms
Homonyms

Week 5 43

from The Lion, The Witch, and The Wardrobe

Noun Review
Common & Proper Nouns
Suffixes: Changing **f** *to* **v**
Synonyms & Antonyms

Week 6 53

October's Party

Noun Review
Plural Possessive Nouns
Noun Titles & Abbreviations
Homonyms
Rhyming Words

Week 7 63

from The Story of the Pilgrim Fathers

The Pronoun
Suffixes: Dropping a Silent **e**
Possessive Nouns & Pronouns
Noun Review

Week 8 73

Come, Ye Thankful People, Come

Compound Words with **full**
Rhyming Pairs
Noun Review
Archaic Pronouns
Homonyms & Antonyms

Week 9 83

from The Burgess Animal Book for Children

Suffixes: One-Syllable Base Word
Noun Review
Past Tense
Onomatopoeia

Week 10 93

from John 1

Suffixes: Two-Syllable Base Word
Noun Review
Spelling Rule: **i** *Before* **e**
Noun & Pronoun Review
Homonyms, Synonyms, & Antonyms

Week 11 103

from A Christmas Carol

Possessive Pronoun **Their** *and Its Homonyms*
Noun Review
Noun & Pronoun Review
Onomatopoeia
Homonyms, Synonyms, & Antonyms

Week 12 113

from Once in Royal David's City

Rhyming Pairs
Noun Review
Possessive Pronouns **Your** *& its Homonyms and* **Whose** *& its Homonyms*
Homonyms, Synonyms, & Antonyms

Materials Needed for Primer Two Autumn

All materials, resources, and links listed below are available at Cottage Press:

www.cottagepress.net

Required

- **Primer Two Teaching Helps** ~ Required to effectively teach all lessons in in Primer. This one book contains teaching helps for all three Primer One student books. It contains instructions for all nature study and picture study lessons, tips and notes for teaching the Spelling, Grammar, and Word Usage lessons, and an answer key for the exercises that warrant it. Teach each lesson in Primer with this book open for ready reference.

- **Primer Resources Webpage** ~ Linked from *cottagepress.net* with many resources for nature and picture study. Bookmark this webpage.

- **Picture Study PDFs** ~ Free, downloadable PDFs for individual artists that include images of selected paintings along with biographical notes and links to many online resources. Available artists include: Audubon, Bruegel, Cassatt, DaVinci, Delacroix, Durer, Homer, Michelangelo, Millet, Monet, Rembrandt, Renoir, Rubens, Stuart, Titian, Van Eyck, Van Gogh, Vermeer. The *Primer Resources Webpage* has links to these free PDFs.

- **Young Folks Treasury: Childhood's Favorites and Fairy Stories** ~ This gem was originally published by the University Society in 1927. All narration selections for *Primer Two Autumn* are found in this book. Purchase a reprint of the 1927 original from the Cottage Press bookstore or download it for free from Project Gutenberg.

    www.gutenberg.org/ebooks/19993

- **Home Geography for Primary Grades, by C.C. Long** ~ This book is used for several nature lessons in each of the *Primer Two* books. Purchase this from the Cottage Press bookstore or download it for free from Project Gutenberg.

    www.gutenberg.org/ebooks/12228

- **A Systematic Phonics and Spelling Program** ~ The lessons in the *Primer* books are designed to reinforce phonics and spelling rules taught in such a program. See recommendations on the *Primer Resources Webpage*.

OPTIONAL
- HIGH QUALITY COLORED PENCILS ~ Prismacolors by Berol are wonderful!
- BOOKS AND RESOURCES FOR THE NATURE AND PICTURE STUDY LESSONS ~ Links to resources (both free and for purchase) are available on the *Primer Resources Webpage*. Check your local library also.

WEEKLY LESSONS

Drawing Page

The Land of Story-Books

At evening when the lamp is lit,
Around the fire my parents sit;
They sit at home and talk and sing,
And do not play at anything.

Now, with my little gun, I crawl
All in the dark along the wall,
And follow round the forest track
Away behind the sofa back.

There, in the night, where none can spy,
All in my hunter's camp I lie,
And play at books that I have read
Till it is time to go to bed.

These are the hills, these are the woods,
These are my starry solitudes;
And there the river by whose brink
The roaring lions come to drink.

I see the others far away
As if in firelit camp they lay,
And I, like to an Indian scout,
Around their party prowled about.

So, when my nurse comes in for me,
Home I return across the sea,
And go to bed with backward looks
At my dear land of Story-books.

~ Robert Louis Stevenson

Week 1 ♦ Day 1

Today is _____
             Day   Date   Year

Read And Narrate

Why the Bear Has a Stumpy Tail
~ *Childhood's Favorites and Fairy Tales*, Edited by Mabie, Hale, and Forbush

Vocabulary to study before you read:

- slinking
- demanded
- bruin
- bade
- smarts

Draw a picture or series of pictures illustrating the story.

Week 1 ◆ Day 1

Copybook

Copy the title and first two stanzas from this week's copybook selection into your copybook. Check your work, word by word, against the original.

Did you

❑ include every word in the original and spell every word correctly?
❑ capitalize every letter that is capitalized in the original?
❑ include every punctuation mark in the original?

Plurals

Make most names of persons, places, things, or ideas plural (more than one) by adding **-s** *or* **-es** *to the base word. There are several words in the exercise below that end with a single vowel* **y**. *In these words, change the* **y** *to an* **i** *and add* **-es.**

Example: **puppy**, change **y → i + es = puppies**

Make these words plural.

lamp	fire	parent
track	wood	party
story	church	box

Writing Sentences

A **sentence** *begins with a capital letter, ends with end punctuation, and expresses a complete thought. In the sentences below, underline the capital letter at the beginning, and circle the end punctuation.*

Home I return across the sea.

I see the others far away.

Week 1 ◆ Day 2

Today is _____
　　　　　　　　　Day　　　　　　　　　　　Date　　　　　　　　　　Year

Nature Study

*Review compass directions with your teacher. Trace over the **compass rose** below. Label the chief (larger) points, starting at the top and working clockwise: **N** (North), **E** (East), **S** (South), **W** (West). Remember the mnemonic **N**ever **E**at **S**hredded **W**heat! Label the lesser points, between the chief points, **NE** (Northeast), **SE** (Southeast), **SW** (Southwest), and **NW** (Northwest).*

On the drawing above, sketch a small picture of your house in the middle of the compass rose. Around the compass rose, sketch small pictures of places that you know (church, grocery store, library, post office, a friend's house, etc.). Place each in its proper relation to your house.

Nature Notebook: Draw a large compass rose. Color and label it. On another page, draw a small compass rose in the lower right hand corner, then do a more detailed and careful picture map of your home and familiar places. Use the compass rose for correct placement of each.

Week 1 ◆ Day 2

Copybook

Copy stanzas three and four from this week's copybook selection into your copybook. Check your work, word by word, against the original.

Did you

❑ include every word in the original and spell every word correctly?
❑ capitalize every letter that is capitalized in the original?
❑ include every punctuation mark in the original?

Days of the Week & Abbreviations

Write the days of the week. Beside each day write its abbreviation by writing the first three letters followed by a period.

Sunday _____

Monday _____

Tuesday _____

Wednesday _____

Thursday _____

Friday _____

Saturday _____

Write two original sentences using one or more days of the week.

_____

_____

_____

WEEK 1 ◆ DAY 3

Today is _____
                      Day   Date   Year

READ AND NARRATE

The Little Red Hen
~ Childhood's Favorites and Fairy Tales, Edited by Mabie, Hale, and Forbush

Vocabulary to study before you read:

grain   ripe   thresh

mill   ground

Draw a picture or series of pictures illustrating the story.

Copybook

Copy the last two stanzas and the attribution from this week's copybook selection into your copybook. The attribution in this case is the name of the poet. Sometimes the attribution will include the book or larger work from which the weekly selection is taken. Check your work, word by word, against the original.

Did you

- ❑ include every word in the original and spell every word correctly?
- ❑ capitalize every letter that is capitalized in the original?
- ❑ include every punctuation mark in the original?

Rhyming Words

Write three words that rhyme with **play**.

Write three words that rhyme with **camp**.

Write three words that rhyme with **time**.

Write an original sentence or two using your rhyming words.

Week 1 ♦ Day 4

Today is _____
                    Day   Date   Year

Picture Study _____

_____

_____

_____

In the space above, make your own rendering of the current work of art using colored pencils, or paste a printout from the Picture Study PDF. Write the title and date of the work on one line, and artist's name below it.

Week 1 • Day 4

Dictation

Months of the Year & Abbreviations

Write the months in order. Beside each month write its abbreviation by writing the first three letters followed by a period.

1.
2.
3.
4.
5.
6.
7.
8.
9.
10.
11.
12.

Drawing Page

from EARLY DAYS IN EGYPT

In the valley of the river Nile, bathed in glittering sunshine, lay the ancient land of Egypt, a narrow strip of green in the midst of the sands of the desert.

From the tall mountains of Central Africa, the Nile cut its way between tall cliffs that glowed rose-pink and lilac, flecked with passing shadows, and lifting clear cut outlines against a bright blue sky.

Six times the river, flowing down on its long way to the sea, halted in its course to swirl in foaming cataracts around obstructing rocks, jagged heaps of black granite, that lay as though hurled by giants across the bed of the stream.

~ Olive Beaupre-Miller, *A Picturesque Tale of Progress, Volume I*

Week 2 ◆ Day 1

Today is _____
                Day   Date   Year

Read And Narrate

Teeny Tiny
~ *Childhood's Favorites and Fairy Tales*, Edited by Mabie, Hale, and Forbush

Vocabulary to study before you read:

village   bonnet   churchyard

cupboard   farther

Draw a picture or series of pictures illustrating the story.

Week 2 ◆ Day 1

Copybook

Copy the title and the first paragraph from this week's copybook selection into your copybook. Check your work, word by word, against the original.

Did you

- ☐ include every word in the original and spell every word correctly?
- ☐ capitalize every letter that is capitalized in the original?
- ☐ include every punctuation mark in the original?

Past Tense

*The past tense ending, **-ed**, added to an action word (a verb), tells us the action happened in the past. It says /**d**/ or /**t**/ unless the word ends in **-d** or **-t**, and then it says /**ed**/.*

Sometimes the past tense is formed by changing the word completely, and sometimes with no change to the word.

Examples: **go → went; hit → hit**

Make these words past tense.

cut	glitter	glow
lift	flow	halt
swirl	hurl	is

Write an original sentence using a past tense verb you formed above.

Week 2 ♦ Day 2

Today is _____
                    Day   Date   Year

Nature Study

Read about about pictures and plans* with your teacher. In the space below, draw a plan of your schoolroom or your bedroom. Add a correctly oriented compass rose.

Nature Notebook: Draw a plan of your house or school and the surrounding streets, fields, etc. Include a compass rose to orient your map correctly.

* See Primer II - Autumn Teaching Helps

Week 2 • Day 2

Copybook

Copy the second paragraph from this week's copybook selection into your copybook. Check your work, word by word, against the original.

Did you

- ❏ include every word in the original and spell every word correctly?
- ❏ capitalize every letter that is capitalized in the original?
- ❏ include every punctuation mark in the original?

Homonyms

Homonyms are words that sound the same, but have different spellings and meanings. **Dear** *and* **deer** *are homonyms.*

Write homonyms for these words.

sun _____

rose _____

blue _____

way _____

to _____

sea _____

Write original sentences using homonyms you wrote above.

_____

_____

_____

Week 2 ◆ Day 3

Today is _____
               Day   *Date*   *Year*

Read And Narrate

The Little Shepherd Boy
~ Childhood's Favorites and Fairy Tales, Edited by Mabie, Hale, and Forbush

Vocabulary to study before you read:

famed	**minute**	**numerous**
dazzled	**whomsoever**	**eternity**
situated	**adamantine**	**breadth**
thither	**sage**	**henceforward**

Draw a picture or series of pictures illustrating the story.

Week 2 • Day 3

Copybook

Copy the last paragraph and the attribution from this week's copybook selection into your copybook. Check your work, word by word, against the original.

Did you

  ❑ include every word in the original and spell every word correctly?
  ❑ capitalize every letter that is capitalized in the original?
  ❑ include every punctuation mark in the original?

Synonyms

Synonyms *are words that have similar meanings; for example, happy is a synonym for glad. Beside each word below write one or more synonyms.*

ancient _____

cut (its way) _____

tall _____

glowed _____

halted _____

hurled _____

Write several original sentences using synonyms you wrote above.

Week 2 • Day 4

Today is _____
                Day   Date   Year

Picture Study _____

_____

_____

_____

Dictation

_____
_____
_____
_____
_____
_____
_____

Plurals

*Make these words plural. There are several words below that end in **-y**, but to make these plural, you just add an **-s**; the **y** does not change to an **i**. Discuss with your teacher why this is so.*

valley	strip	desert
mountain	cliff	shadow
cataract	joy	way

Write an original sentence with one of the plural words you wrote above.

_____
_____

DRAWING PAGE

from Psalm 27

¹The Lord is my light and my salvation—
  whom shall I fear?
The Lord is the stronghold of my life—
  of whom shall I be afraid?

²When the wicked advance against me
  to devour me,
it is my enemies and my foes
  who will stumble and fall.
³Though an army besiege me,
  my heart will not fear;
though war break out against me,
  even then I will be confident.

⁴One thing I ask from the Lord,
  this only do I seek:
that I may dwell in the house of the Lord
  all the days of my life,
to gaze on the beauty of the Lord
  and to seek him in his temple.
⁵For in the day of trouble
  he will keep me safe in his dwelling;
he will hide me in the shelter of his sacred tent
  and set me high upon a rock.

~ Psalm 27:1-5, New King James Version

Week 3 ◆ Day 1

Today is _____
　　　　　　　　Day　　　　　　　　　Date　　　　　　　　Year

How to Tell a True Princess
~ *Childhood's Favorites and Fairy Tales*, Edited by Mabie, Hale, and Forbush

Vocabulary to study before you read:

defect	genuine	article
low spirits	torrents	plight
eider-down	perceived	sensitive

Draw a picture or series of pictures illustrating the story.

Week 3 • Day 1

Copybook

Copy the title and the first verse from this week's copybook selection into your copybook. Check your work, word by word, against the original.

Did you

- ☐ include every word in the original and spell every word correctly?
- ☐ capitalize every letter that is capitalized in the original?
- ☐ include every punctuation mark in the original?

The Noun

George Washington, grandmother, *and* shopkeeper *are words that* **name** *persons.* Virginia, river, *and* kitchen *are words that* **name** *places.* Blackboard, tail, *and* blanket *are words that* **name** *things.* Life, love, *and* happiness *are words that* **name** *ideas. A* **noun** *is a word that* **names** *a person, place, thing, or idea.*

Here is a list of nouns from this week's copybook selection:

Lord, light, salvation, foes, house, beauty, tent, rock

Write the two nouns from the list that name persons:

_____

Write the two nouns from the list that name places:

_____

Write the two nouns from the list that name things:

_____

Write the two nouns from the list that name ideas:

_____

Week 3 ◆ Day 2

Today is _____
                Day   *Date*   *Year*

Nature Study

Read about about plains, hills, mountains, and valleys* with your teacher. In the frame below, sketch a **landscape** *which includes all of these.*

Nature Notebook: Copy and color your landscape drawing, adding additional detail to make a beautiful picture.

*   See Primer II - Autumn Teaching Helps

Week 3 • Day 2

Copybook

Copy the second and third verses from this week's copybook selection into your copybook. Check your work, word by word, against the original.

Did you

- ☐ include every word in the original and spell every word correctly?
- ☐ capitalize every letter that is capitalized in the original?
- ☐ include every punctuation mark in the original?

Spelling Rule: I Before E

*Use **i** before **e**, except after **c**, and when it says /ā/ as in **neighbor**. There are some exceptions to this rule, but since **ie** is the most common usage when these two letters are paired, it is a helpful rule to know. Read and copy these words.*

| besiege | chief | believe |

| shriek | pierce | shield |

Here are a few exceptions you should memorize. Copy these also.

| either | neither | height |

| seize | leisure | foreign |

Rhyming Words

*Write three words that rhyme with **seek**.*

Week 3 ♦ Day 3

Today is _____
                  Day   Date   Year

READ AND NARRATE

The Miller, His Son, and Their Ass
~ Childhood's Favorites and Fairy Tales, Edited by Mabie, Hale, and Forbush

Vocabulary to study before you read:

miller	ass	dame
tramped	merrily	rascal
idle	hardly	load
slung	jeered	

Draw a picture or series of pictures illustrating the story.

Week 3 • Day 3

Copybook

Copy the fourth and fifth verses and the attribution from this week's copybook selection into your copybook. Check your work, word by word, against the original.

Did you

- ☐ include every word in the original and spell every word correctly?
- ☐ capitalize every letter that is capitalized in the original?
- ☐ include every punctuation mark in the original?

Antonyms

*Antonyms are words that have opposite meanings, like **happy** and **sad**. Beside each word below write one or more antonyms.*

wicked _____

enemies _____

light _____

Homonyms & Synonyms

Write a homonym for each of these words.

days _____

Write one or more synonyms for each of these words.

wicked _____

enemies _____

dwell _____

Week 3 ◆ Day 4

Today is _____
                    Day   *Date*   *Year*

P<small>ICTURE</small> S<small>TUDY</small>

Dictation

_____
_____
_____
_____
_____
_____

Past Tense & Plural

Make these words past tense.

| advance | fall | break |

| reside | seek | keep |

Make these nouns plural.

| army | day | beauty |

Write an original sentence using several of the words you wrote above.

_____
_____

Drawing Page

from THE REAL PRINCESS

One evening a fearful tempest arose, it thundered and lightened, and the rain poured down from the sky in torrents: besides, it was as dark as pitch. All at once there was heard a violent knocking at the door, and the old King, the Prince's father, went out himself to open it.

It was a Princess who was standing outside the door. What with the rain and the wind, she was in a sad condition; the water trickled down from her hair, and her clothes clung to her body. She said she was a real Princess.

"Ah! we shall soon see that!" thought the old Queen-mother; however, she said not a word of what she was going to do; but went quietly into the bedroom, took all the bed-clothes off the bed, and put three little peas on the bedstead. She then laid twenty mattresses one upon another over the three peas, and put twenty feather beds over the mattresses.

~ Hans Christian Andersen

Week 4 ◆ Day 1

Today is _____
             Day   Date   Year

The Spider and the Flea
~ *Childhood's Favorites and Fairy Tales*, Edited by Mabie, Hale, and Forbush

Vocabulary to study before you read:

dwelt	brewed	scalded
thereupon	industriously	presently
furiously	maiden	streamlet

Draw a picture or series of pictures illustrating the story.

Week 4 ◆ Day 1

Copybook

Copy the title, and the first paragraph from this week's copybook selection into your copybook. Check your work, word by word, against the original.

Did you

❑ include every word in the original and spell every word correctly?

❑ capitalize every letter that is capitalized in the original?

❑ include every punctuation mark in the original?

Noun Review

From this week's selection, write two nouns that name persons:

_____

_____

From this week's selection, write two nouns that name things:

_____

_____

Possessive Nouns

An apostrophe (') + s is added to a noun to show ownership.

John's hat = the hat belonging to John

One noun in this week's copybook selection is possessive. Write it below.

_____

Write one sentence below using the possessive noun you wrote above. Include the thing possessed.

Example: The Queen's plan was carried out.

_____

_____

Week 4 ♦ Day 2

Today is _____
           Day   Date   Year

Nature Study

Read about about rivers* with your teacher. In the frame below, sketch the path from a mountain stream to an ocean. Include a stream or brook, a river, and the ocean.

Nature Notebook: Draw and color a more detailed drawing of stream to ocean.

* See Primer II - Autumn Teaching Helps

36

Week 4 • Day 2

Copybook

Copy the second paragraph from this week's copybook selection into your copybook. Check your work, word by word, against the original.

Did you

❏ include every word in the original and spell every word correctly?
❏ capitalize every letter that is capitalized in the original?
❏ include every punctuation mark in the original?

Singular & Plural Nouns

*When a noun names only one person, place, thing, or idea, we say that it is **singular**. When it names two or more, we say that it is **plural**.*

From this week's selection, write three nouns that are plural:

_____

Make these nouns plural.

tempest	rain	sky
wind	father	Princess
mattress	feather	pea

Rewrite the sentence below, but change the underlined word to a plural noun. You will have to make some adjustments to other words in the sentence so that your new sentence makes complete sense.

A <u>Princess</u> was standing outside the door.

_____

37

Week 4 • Day 3

Today is _____
           Day   Date   Year

Read And Narrate _____

The Elves and the Shoemaker
~ *Childhood's Favorites and Fairy Tales*, Edited by Mabie, Hale, and Forbush

Vocabulary to study before you read:

intended	conscience	examine
purchaser	ordinary	lacking
circumstances	lends	swiftly
gratitude	excessively	cobble
fared	undertakings	

Draw a picture or series of pictures illustrating the story.

Copybook

Copy the third paragraph and the attribution from this week's copybook selection into your copybook. Check your work, word by word, against the original.

Did you

- ❑ include every word in the original and spell every word correctly?
- ❑ capitalize every letter that is capitalized in the original?
- ❑ include every punctuation mark in the original?

Synonyms & Antonyms

Write one or more synonyms for each of these words.

violent _____

real _____

Write one or more antonyms for each of these words.

violent _____

real _____

Homonyms

Write a homonym for each of these words.

heard _____

hair _____

*Write an original sentence using the homonym for **hair**.*

_____

Week 4 ◆ Day 4

Today is _____
             Day   Date   Year

Picture Study _____

_____

_____

_____

40

Dictation

_____
_____
_____
_____
_____
_____

Simile

A **simile** compares two things that are not usually associated with one another by using the words *like, as,* or *than.*

> Her smile was *like* sunshine. Her smile was bright *as* sunshine. Her smile was brighter *than* sunshine.

In these examples, her smile is compared to sunshine.

Find the simile in this week's copybook selection. Write the two things being compared.

_____ is compared to _____

Authors use similes to help you imagine what they are describing—to actually see a picture in your mind. Look and listen for similes in your reading this week, and write them here if you find any.

_____
_____
_____

DRAWING PAGE

from THE LION, THE WITCH, AND THE WARDROBE

Once there were four children whose names were Peter, Susan, Edmund, and Lucy. This story is about something that happened to them when they were sent away from London during the war because of the air-raids. They were sent to the house of an old Professor who lived in the heart of the country, ten miles from the nearest post office. He had no wife and he lived in a very large house with a housekeeper called Mrs. Macready and three servants. (Their names were Ivy, Margaret, and Betty, but they do not come into the story much.) He himself was a very old man with shaggy white hair which grew over most of his face as well as on his head, and they liked him almost at once; but on the first evening when he came out to meet them at the front door he was so odd-looking that Lucy (who was the youngest) was a little afraid of him, and Edmund (who was the next youngest) wanted to laugh and had to keep on pretending he was blowing his nose to hide it.

As soon as they had said good night to the Professor and gone upstairs on the first night, the boys came into the girls' room and they all talked it over.

"We've fallen on our feet and no mistake," said Peter. "This is going to be perfectly splendid. That old chap will let us do anything we like."

~ C. S. Lewis

Week 5 ♦ Day 1

Today is _____
                      Day   *Date*   *Year*

Chicken-Licken

~ *Childhood's Favorites and Fairy Tales*, Edited by Mabie, Hale, and Forbush

Vocabulary to study before you read:

cock   drake   gander

Draw a picture or series of pictures illustrating the story.

Week 5 ◆ Day 1

COPYBOOK

Copy the title and half of the first paragraph from this week's copybook selection into your copybook. Check your work, word by word, against the original.

Did you

- ❏ include every word in the original and spell every word correctly?
- ❏ capitalize every letter that is capitalized in the original?
- ❏ include every punctuation mark in the original?

NOUN REVIEW

From this week's copybook selection, write four nouns that name places:

_____

_____

Make these nouns possessive.

Peter	Professor	house
man	child	country

Which of these nouns are singular? Which are plural? Make the singular nouns plural, and the plural nouns singular.

children	house	country
servants	man	boys

45

Week 5 ♦ Day 2

Today is _____
                Day   Date   Year

Nature Study

Read about maps[1] with your teacher. In each of the frames below, draw a map to illustrate the geographical term listed below it.

Bay

Peninsula

Strait

Isthmus

Nature Notebook: Draw and illustrate a map. Include a compass rose for orientation. It can be a map you copy from a book or atlas, or your own original for a real or imaginary place.

1 See Primer II - Autumn Teaching Helps

Week 5 • Day 2

Copybook

Finish copying the first paragraph from this week's copybook selection into your copybook. Check your work, word by word, against the original.

Did you

- ☐ include every word in the original and spell every word correctly?
- ☐ capitalize every letter that is capitalized in the original?
- ☐ include every punctuation mark in the original?

Common & Proper Nouns

Nouns that name particular persons, places, things, and ideas are called **proper nouns**. *Proper nouns are always capitalized. Nouns that are common to a group of persons, places, things, or ideas are called* **common nouns**.

Here is a list of nouns from this week's copybook selection:

Peter, house, Lucy, man, Edmund, chap, servants, Susan, Professor, country, Mrs. Macready, London

From the list above, write the six proper nouns that name particular persons.

_____

_____

From the list above, write the proper noun that names a particular place.

_____

From the list above, write the three common nouns that name persons.

_____

From the list above, write the two common nouns that name places.

_____

Week 5 ♦ Day 3

Today is _____
                Day   Date   Year

Read And Narrate

The Three Brothers
~ Childhood's Favorites and Fairy Tales, Edited by Mabie, Hale, and Forbush

Vocabulary to study before you read:

fond	forefathers	handicraft
content	farrier	fencing
thoroughly	shod	certainly
lather	astonished	satisfied
devoted	grieved	pined

Draw a picture or series of pictures illustrating the story.

Copybook

Copy the final two paragraphs and the attribution from this week's copybook selection into your copybook. Check your work, word by word, against the original.

Did you

- ❏ include every word in the original and spell every word correctly?
- ❏ capitalize every letter that is capitalized in the original?
- ❏ include every punctuation mark in the original

Suffixes: Changing F to V

There words in the exercise below end with the sound of **f**. In some words that end with a single consonant **f** (sometimes followed by a silent **e**), the **-f** (or the **-fe**) changes to **v** and then you add **-es**.

Example: leaf, change **f** → **v** + **es** = **leaves**

Write an **S** beside the nouns below that are singular, and a **P** for those that are plural. Make the plural nouns singular, and the singular nouns plural.

wife	calves	lives
loaf	knife	wolves

The words below also end with the sound of **f**. These words do not change when we make them plural. Write the plural of these words by just adding an **-s**.

cliff	chief	roof

Now, go back and say each word and its plural. In the words that have a change from **f** to **v**, you can hear the **v** sound when you say the plural. The words with no change continue to say the **f** sound in their plural forms. This is a case where you have to listen carefully to proper pronunciation in order to spell correctly!

Week 5 • Day 4

Today is _____
   Day   Date   Year

PICTURE STUDY

Week 5 ♦ Day 4

Dictation

_____
_____
_____
_____
_____
_____
_____

Synonyms & Antonyms

Write one or more synonyms for each of these words.

man   _____

splendid   _____

Write one or more antonyms for each of these words.

liked   _____

splendid   _____

Write an original sentence using one of the synonyms and one of the antonyms you wrote above.

_____
_____

DRAWING PAGE

October's Party

October gave a party;
    The leaves by hundreds came —
The Chestnuts, Oaks, and Maples,
    And leaves of every name.
The Sunshine spread a carpet,
    And everything was grand,
Miss Weather led the dancing,
    Professor Wind the band.

The Chestnuts came in yellow,
    The Oaks in crimson dressed;
The lovely Misses Maple
    In scarlet looked their best;
All balanced to their partners,
    And gaily fluttered by;
The sight was like a rainbow
    New fallen from the sky.

Then, in the rustic hollow,
    At hide-and-seek they played,
The party closed at sundown,
    And everybody stayed.
Professor Wind played louder;
    They flew along the ground;
And then the party ended
    In jolly "hands around."

~ George Cooper

Week 6 ◆ Day 1

Today is _____
           Day   Date   Year

Read And Narrate
_____

Toads and Diamonds
~ *Childhood's Favorites and Fairy Tales*, Edited by Mabie, Hale, and Forbush

Vocabulary to study before you read:

disposition	amiable	doted
compelled	leavings	infirm
slaked	issued	forlorn
civilly	menial	sullenly
discourtesy	breeding	enraptured

Draw a picture or series of pictures illustrating the story.

Week 6 ♦ Day 1

Copybook

Copy the title and the first stanza from this week's copybook selection into your copybook. Check your work, word by word, against the original.

Did you

- ☐ include every word in the original and spell every word correctly?
- ☐ capitalize every letter that is capitalized in the original?
- ☐ include every punctuation mark in the original?

Noun Review

In this poem, the particular month *of October gives a party. This party is attended by a particular* wind *and a particular* sunshine, *and leaves from particular* trees. *The poet wants us to think of these things as particular* persons, *so he makes them into* **proper nouns.** *Because they are proper nouns, they must be capitalized.*

Write the seven proper nouns used in the first stanza.

_____

_____

_____

From this week's copybook selection, write four common nouns. For each noun you write, tell your teacher which it names: person, place, thing, or idea.

_____

_____

Write an original sentence using one of the common nouns and one of the proper nouns you wrote above.

_____

_____

Week 6 • Day 2

Today is _____
                         Day   Date   Year

NATURE STUDY

Tree Observation: Draw the leaf and the seed in the frame below.

Identify the tree, and write the English and Latin names:

_____

_____

Nature Notebook: Draw the tree from which you retrieved this leaf. Write its English and Latin name, and include a smaller sketch of the leaf and seed.

Week 6 ♦ Day 2

Copybook

Copy the second stanza from this week's copybook selection into your copybook. Check your work, word by word, against the original.

Did you

- ☐ include every word in the original and spell every word correctly?
- ☐ capitalize every letter that is capitalized in the original?
- ☐ include every punctuation mark in the original?

Plural Possessive Nouns

One noun in this week's copybook selection is possessive. Write it below.

_____

_____

To form the possessive of *plural words ending in -s*, add the apostrophe (') alone:

    Example: *bunnies' shoes; birds' nests*

Write the alternate possessive forms below.

flight of leaves   _____

dresses of Oaks   _____

games of children   _____

music of bands   _____

carpet of Sunshine   _____

Write one sentence below using one of the possessive noun you wrote above. Be sure to include the thing possessed.

_____

_____

Week 6 • Day 3

Today is _____
                Day   Date   Year

The Wolf and The Fox
~ Childhood's Favorites and Fairy Tales, Edited by Mabie, Hale, and Forbush

Vocabulary to study before you read:

fetch	proposal	awkwardly
aroused	bleat	glutton
covetous	dispatched	hastening
lame	cask	condition
abundance	cunningly	cudgel

Draw a picture or series of pictures illustrating the story.

Week 6 • Day 3

Copybook

Copy the third stanza and the attribution from this week's copybook selection into your copybook. Check your work, word by word, against the original.

Did you

❑ include every word in the original and spell every word correctly?
❑ capitalize every letter that is capitalized in the original?
❑ include every punctuation mark in the original?

Noun Titles & Abbreviations

Titles like Mister, Mistress, and Doctor are often abbreviated. Write the abbreviations for these titles. Ask your teacher for help if you do not know the correct abbreviation.

Mister	_____	Mistress	_____
Saint	_____	Professor	_____
Reverend	_____	Doctor	_____
Captain	_____	General	_____

The title Miss is not abbreviated. Titles are often paired with a name to form a proper noun. Notice how the title Miss for the two (or more) young Maple ladies is made plural. Write the proper noun (plural title plus the name) below:

_____

To make these compound terms plural, you may pluralize the title as in the copybook selection, or you may pluralize the abbreviation. For example, Mr. Smith and his wife are both doctors, so we might write a sentence about them like one of these:

The Doctors Smith are in the office. The Drs. Smith are in the office.

Write a short sentence about two Professors, both named Wind.

Week 6 ~ Day 4

Today is _____
　　　　　　　　　Day　　　　　　　*Date*　　　　　　*Year*

Picture Study _____

Week 6 • Day 4

Dictation

Homonyms

Beside the word below write a homonym.

by _____

new _____

Simile

Find the simile in this week's copybook selection. Remember that a simile must use the words like, as, or than. Write the two things being compared.

_____ is compared to _____

Rhyming Words

*Write three words that rhyme with **oak**.*

Drawing Page

from THE STORY OF THE PILGRIM FATHERS

The weather was bitterly cold and the frost so keen that even their clothes were frozen stiff. And ere these Pilgrims could find a shelter from the winter blasts, trees had to be felled and hewn for the building of their houses. It was enough to make the stoutest heart quake. Yet not one among this little band of Pilgrims flinched or thought of turning back. They were made of sterner stuff than that, and they put all their trust in God.

The first winter the Pilgrim Fathers, it was said, "endured a wonderful deal of misery with infinite patience." But at length spring came, and with the coming of warmth and sunshine the sickness disappeared. The sun seemed to put new life into every one. So when in April the Mayflower, which had been in harbour all winter, sailed homeward not one of the Pilgrims sailed with her.

What was their surprise then when one morning an Indian walked boldly into the camp and spoke to them in broken English!

He told them that his name was Samoset, and that he was the Englishmen's friend. He also said he could tell them of another Indian called Squanto who could speak better English than he could. This Squanto had been stolen away from his home by a wicked captain who intended to sell him as a slave to Spain. But he had escaped to England, and later by the help of Englishmen had been brought back to his home. All his tribe however had meantime been swept away by a plague, and now only he remained.

~ *This Country of Ours*, H.E. Marshall

Week 7 ◆ Day 1

Today is _____
              Day   Date   Year

Singh Rajah and the Three Cunning Jackals
~ *Childhood's Favorites and Fairy Tales*, Edited by Mabie, Hale, and Forbush

Vocabulary to study before you read:

rajah	subjects	ranee
manage	wretches	dale
lashed	gnashed	creeping
bidding	supreme	defiant
rage	treacherous	

Draw a picture or series of pictures illustrating the story.

Week 7 ♦ Day 1

Copybook

Copy the title and the first paragraph from this week's copybook selection into your copybook. Check your work, word by word, against the original.

Did you

- ☐ include every word in the original and spell every word correctly?
- ☐ capitalize every letter that is capitalized in the original?
- ☐ include every punctuation mark in the original?

The Pronoun

*A **pronoun** is a word that stands in for a noun.*

> *The Pilgrims trusted God. The Mayflower sailed, but the Pilgrims remained.*
>
> *They trusted Him. She sailed, but they remained.*

In the second set of sentences above: They *is a pronoun standing in for Pilgrims;* Him *is a pronoun standing in for God;* She *is a pronoun standing in for the Mayflower;* they *is a pronoun standing in for the Pilgrims. (Do you know why we use* she *instead of* it *to stand in for a ship? Talk with your teacher about this.)*

Pronouns are words like I, you, he, she, it, we, they, me, my, your, him, his, her, us, that, this, them, himself, herself, itself. *Rewrite each of these sentences, substituting an appropriate pronoun for the underlined word.*

The Pilgrims felled trees and used trees to build houses.

The Mayflower sailed, but not one of the Pilgrims sailed with the Mayflower.

The plague swept the tribe away, and Squanto alone remained.

Week 7 • Day 2

Today is _____
            Day   Date   Year

NATURE STUDY

Tree Observation: Draw the leaf and the seed in the frame below.

[ ]

Identify the tree, and write the English and Latin names:

_____

_____

Nature Notebook: Draw the tree from which you retrieved this leaf. Write its English and Latin name, and include a smaller sketch of the leaf and seed.

Week 7 • Day 2

COPYBOOK

Copy the second paragraph from this week's copybook selection into your copybook. Check your work, word by word, against the original.

Did you

❑ include every word in the original and spell every word correctly?
❑ capitalize every letter that is capitalized in the original?
❑ include every punctuation mark in the original?

SUFFIXES: DROPPING A SILENT E

Words that end with a silent **e** drop the **e** when adding a suffix that begins with a vowel. Add the suffix **-ing** to these words.

clothe	quake	endure
come	surprise	name
make	slave	escape

Make these words past tense. Some just add **-ed**. Some drop the silent **e** at the end and add **-ed**. Some change completely. One not change at all.

clothe	quake	think
make	endure	seem
put	walk	sweep

Week 7 • Day 3

Today is _____
                Day   Date   Year

Read And Narrate

The Greedy Brownie
~ Childhood's Favorites and Fairy Tales, Edited by Mabie, Hale, and Forbush

Vocabulary to study before you read:

hollow	laird	thistles
doze	weary	disturbed
lassies	espied	delicacy
quarreling	guiltily	basin
supped	bewildered	

Draw a picture or series of pictures illustrating the story.

Week 7 ♦ Day 3

Copybook

Copy the third paragraph and the attribution from this week's copybook selection into your copybook. Check your work, word by word, against the original.

Did you

- ❑ include every word in the original and spell every word correctly?
- ❑ capitalize every letter that is capitalized in the original?
- ❑ include every punctuation mark in the original?

Possessive Nouns & Pronouns

One noun in this week's copybook selection is possessive. Write it below, along with the thing possessed. Is the possessive noun singular or plural?

___

Pronouns can also be possessive. Write the missing possessive form below.

houses of them	their houses
trust of us	
English of him	
sails of her	

One very important rule to remember: **Possessive pronouns NEVER use an apostrophe.** The most commonly misused plural possessive pronoun is *its*. When it has an apostrophe followed by an **s**, it actually indicates a contraction:

It's raining = It is raining.

Copy this sentence which uses *its* correctly.

Spring came, bringing its warmth and sunshine.

Week 7 • Day 4

Today is _____
                        Day   *Date*   *Year*

Picture Study

Week 7 • Day 4

Dictation

Noun Review

Write four proper nouns used in the final paragraph of this week's copybook selection.

Write four common nouns used in the first paragraph of this week's copybook selection.

Tell your teacher whether each noun you wrote above names a person, place, thing, or idea. Tell whether each is singular or plural.

Beside the nouns below write one or more synonyms.

houses

surprise

Drawing Page

COME, YE THANKFUL PEOPLE, COME

Come, ye thankful people, come,
Raise the song of harvest home!
All is safely gathered in,
Ere the winter storms begin;
God, our Maker, doth provide
For our wants to be supplied;
Come to God's own temple, come;
Raise the song of harvest home!

We ourselves are God's own field,
Fruit unto His praise to yield;
Wheat and tares together sown
Unto joy or sorrow grown;
First the blade and then the ear,
Then the full corn shall appear;
Lord of harvest, grant that we
Wholesome grain and pure may be.

For the Lord our God shall come,
And shall take the harvest home;
From His field shall in that day
All offenses purge away,
Give His angels charge at last
In the fire the tares to cast;
But the fruitful ears to store
In His garner evermore.

Even so, Lord quickly come,
To Thy final harvest home;
Gather Thou Thy people in,
Free from sorrow, free from sin,
There, forever purified,
In Thy presence to abide;
Come, with all Thine angels, come,
Raise the glorious harvest home!

~ Henry Alford

Week 8 ◆ Day 1

Today is _____
                    Day   *Date*   *Year*

The Three Spinners
~ *Childhood's Favorites and Fairy Tales*, Edited by Mabie, Hale, and Forbush

Vocabulary to study before you read:

ashamed	afford	flax
account	industry	dowry
consequence	admitted	trod
moistened	concealed	commenced
exceedingly	consented	relations

Draw a picture or series of pictures illustrating the story.

Week 8 ◆ Day 1

Copybook

Copy the title and the first stanza from this week's copybook selection into your copybook. Check your work, word by word, against the original.

Did you

- ❏ include every word in the original and spell every word correctly?
- ❏ capitalize every letter that is capitalized in the original?
- ❏ include every punctuation mark in the original?

Compound Words with **Full**

When **full** is added to another word to make a new compound word, it is spelled with just one **l**.

thank + full = _____   (full of thanks)

joy + full = _____   (full of joy)

sorrow + full = _____   (full of sorrow)

fruit + full = _____   (full of fruit)

Rhyming Pairs

This hymn is written with three pairs of rhyming words at the end of the lines of each stanza. Notice that in most of the rhyming pairs, the endings of both words are spelled the same way, like **field** and **yield**. But in some pairs, the endings of both words are spelled differently, like **provide** and **supplied**. Write the other pair of rhyming words in the copybook selection which has endings that are spelled differently.

_____

_____

Write several words that rhyme with **grown**. At least one of them should have an ending that is spelled differently.

_____

_____

Week 8 • Day 2

Today is _____
                  Day   Date   Year

Nature Study

Tree Observation: Draw the leaf and the seed in the frame below.

[ ]

Identify the tree, and write the English and Latin names:

_____

_____

Nature Notebook: Draw the tree from which you retrieved this leaf. Write its English and Latin name, and include a smaller sketch of the leaf and seed.

Week 8 ♦ Day 2

Copybook

Copy the second and third stanzas from this week's copybook selection into your copybook. Check your work, word by word, against the original.

Did you

- ☐ include every word in the original and spell every word correctly?
- ☐ capitalize every letter that is capitalized in the original?
- ☐ include every punctuation mark in the original?

Noun Review

From this week's copybook selection:

Write three proper nouns that name particular persons.

_____

Write three common nouns that name places.

_____

Write three common nouns that name things.

_____

Write three common nouns that name ideas.

_____

From the first stanza of the poem, write the plural common noun which names persons. Write the singular form after it. Use the singular form in a short original sentence.

_____

_____

Week 8 ♦ Day 3

Today is _____
　　　　　　　　Day　　　　　　　　Date　　　　　　　Year

Read And Narrate _____

Discreet Hans
~ *Childhood's Favorites and Fairy Tales*, Edited by Mabie, Hale, and Forbush

Vocabulary to study before you read:

discreet　　　　　　whither　　　　　　foolishly

suffocated　　　　　calf　　　　　　　made sheep's eyes

Draw a picture or series of pictures illustrating the story.

Week 8 • Day 3

Copybook

Copy the fourth stanza and the attribution from this week's copybook selection into your copybook. Check your work, word by word, against the original.

Did you

- ☐ include every word in the original and spell every word correctly?
- ☐ capitalize every letter that is capitalized in the original?
- ☐ include every punctuation mark in the original?

Archaic Pronouns

*This hymn has several pronouns that we do not often use today: ye, thou, thy and thine. We call these **archaic pronouns**. The word archaic means "from an earlier period of time". These pronouns are often used in hymns and prayers, because they were in common usage when the King James version of the Bible was written. Today, instead of thou and ye we say you; instead of thy and thine we say your.*

Rewrite the sentence below. For the underlined noun, substitute an appropriate pronoun. For the underlined pronoun, substitute the appropriate noun.

<u>His</u> thankful people are <u>God's</u> own field.

Write the alternate possessive form below, along with the thing possessed.

wants of us   _____

temple of God   _____

praise of Him   _____

people of Thine   _____

presence of You   _____

home of it   _____

79

Week 8 ◆ Day 4

Today is _____
　　　　　　　　　Day　　　　　　　　　*Date*　　　　　　　　　*Year*

Picture Study _____

Dictation

_____

_____

_____

_____

_____

_____

Homonyms & Antonyms

Write a homonym for each word below.

in   _____

tares   _____

Write one or more antonyms for each word below.

joy   _____

wheat   _____

Write an original sentence or two. Use at least one of the homonyms and one of the antonyms which you wrote above in each.

_____

_____

_____

Week 8 • Day 4

Drawing Page

from THE BURGESS ANIMAL BOOK FOR CHILDREN

Peter had been looking along that little ridge and had discovered that it ended only a short distance from him. Now as he looked at it again, he saw the flat surface of the ground at the end of the ridge rise as if being pushed up from beneath, and that little ridge became just so much longer. Peter understood perfectly. Out of sight beneath the surface Miner the Mole was at work. He was digging a tunnel, and that ridge was simply the roof to that tunnel. It was so near the surface of the ground that Miner simply pushed up the loose soil as he bored his way along, and this made the little ridge over which Peter had stumbled.

Peter watched a few minutes, then turned and scampered, lipperty-lipperty-lip, for the Green Forest. He arrived at school quite out of breath, the last one. Old Mother Nature was about to chide him for being late, but noticing his excitement, she changed her mind.

"Well, Peter," said she. "What is it now? Did you have a narrow escape on your way here?"

~ Thornton Burgess

Week 9 ◆ Day 1

Today is _____
              Day   Date   Year

The Tale of Peter Rabbit
~ Childhood's Favorites and Fairy Tales, Edited by Mabie, Hale, and Forbush

Vocabulary to study before you read:

mischief	currant	gooseberry
implored	exert	sieve
upsetting	damp	wander
twitched	hoe	fortnight

Draw a picture or series of pictures illustrating the story.

Week 9 • Day 1

Copybook

Copy the title and first paragraph from this week's copybook selection into your copybook. Check your work, word by word, against the original.

Did you

☐ include every word in the original and spell every word correctly?
☐ capitalize every letter that is capitalized in the original?
☐ include every punctuation mark in the original?

Suffixes: One-Syllable Base Word

*When adding a suffix beginning with a vowel to a one-syllable word, double the final consonant if the word ends in one vowel then one consonant that you can see AND hear. (Note: when a word ends in **x**, how many consonants do you HEAR?)*

*Add **-ing** to these words.*

dig	sin	sun
hop	track	fix
rise	work	push
stumble	arrive	chide

Choose two of the words you wrote above, and use them in an original sentence.

Week 9 • Day 2

Today is _____
           Day   Date   Year

Nature Study

Review the characteristics of mammals:

- ✓ have a backbone (vertebrates)
- ✓ are warm-blooded
- ✓ have lungs that breathe air
- ✓ have hair
- ✓ most give birth to live young
- ✓ feed their young with milk

List ten mammals below.

1. _____
2. _____
3. _____
4. _____
5. _____
6. _____
7. _____
8. _____
9. _____
10. _____

Week 9 • Day 2

Copybook

Copy the second paragraph from this week's copybook selection into your copybook. Check your work, word by word, against the original.

Did you

❑ include every word in the original and spell every word correctly?

❑ capitalize every letter that is capitalized in the original?

❑ include every punctuation mark in the original?

Noun Review

From this week's copybook selection:

Write three proper nouns that name particular persons.

_____

Write the proper noun that names a place.

_____

Write three common nouns that name places.

_____

For each of the singular nouns below, write the plural form; for each of the plural nouns, write the singular form.

ridge   sight   minutes

_____

push   roof   escapes

_____

Week 9 ♦ Day 3

Today is _____
           Day   Date   Year

Read And Narrate

The Three Bears
~ *Childhood's Favorites and Fairy Tales*, Edited by Mabie, Hale, and Forbush

Vocabulary to study before you read:

hearthrug	meddling	mischievous
resist	trotted	whilst
smelt	suited	outright
smothered	cross	coverlet
rumpled		

Draw a picture or series of pictures illustrating the story.

Copybook

Copy the third paragraph and the attribution from this week's copybook selection into your copybook. Check your work, word by word, against the original.

Did you

❑ include every word in the original and spell every word correctly?
❑ capitalize every letter that is capitalized in the original?
❑ include every punctuation mark in the original?

Past Tense

Make these words past tense.

look	rise	understand
dig	bore	stumble
watch	scamper	notice
chide	hop	skip

Write two original sentences using at least one of the past tense words you wrote above in each sentence.

Week 9 ◆ Day 4

Today is _____
                        Day   Date   Year

Picture Study _____

Dictation

Write the second paragraph from dictation.

_____

_____

_____

_____

_____

_____

Onomatopoeia

In this week's copybook selection, we find the delightful phrase lipperty-lipperty-lip. *This is a figure of speech called* **onomatopoeia** *(pronounced ah-nah-MAH-tah-pē-yah). In onomatopoeia, the spelling or sound of the word gives us a clue to the meaning. The author's use of* lipperty-lipperty-lip *helps us to hear the sound Peter makes as he scampers along. Sometimes onomatopoiea words are actually imitations of a particular sound, such as* oink *or* splash. *Write an onomatopoeia word for the following:*

the sound a cat makes   _____

the sound a bee makes   _____

the sound a snake makes   _____

the sound a lion makes   _____

the sound a brook makes   _____

a baby's sound of delight   _____

Drawing Page

from JOHN 1

In the beginning was the Word, and the Word was with God, and the Word was God. He was in the beginning with God. All things were made through Him, and without Him nothing was made that was made. In Him was life, and the life was the light of men. And the light shines in the darkness, and the darkness did not comprehend it.

He was in the world, and the world was made through Him, and the world did not know Him. He came to His own, and His own did not receive Him. But as many as received Him, to them He gave the right to become children of God, to those who believe in His name: who were born, not of blood, nor of the will of the flesh, nor of the will of man, but of God.

And the Word became flesh and dwelt among us, and we beheld His glory, the glory as of the only begotten of the Father, full of grace and truth.

~ John 1: 1-4, 10-14, New King James Version

Week 10 • Day 1

Today is _____
                    Day   Date   Year

The Musicians of Bremen
~ Childhood's Favorites and Fairy Tales, Edited by Mabie, Hale, and Forbush

Vocabulary to study before you read:

well-nigh	lute	nocturnal
vagabonds	marrow	prophesy
latter	pasturage	counsel
contrive	panes	precipitation
extinguished	reconnoiter	knave

Draw a picture or series of pictures illustrating the story.

Week 10 ♦ Day 1

Copybook

Copy the title and first paragraph from this week's copybook selection into your copybook. Check your work, word by word, against the original.

Did you

❑ include every word in the original and spell every word correctly?
❑ capitalize every letter that is capitalized in the original?
❑ include every punctuation mark in the original?

Suffixes: Two-Syllable Base Word

When adding a suffix beginning with a vowel to a two-syllable word, double the final consonant if

✓ the word ends in one vowel then one consonant that you can see AND hear
✓ the accent is on the last syllable of the base word

Add **-ing** to these words.

begin	beget	forget
control	prefer	excel
travel	profit	annoy

Choose two of the words you wrote above, and use them in an original sentence.

Week 10 • Day 2

Today is _____
                          Day   Date   Year

NATURE STUDY

Choose a mammal, and talk about its characteristics, covering the points below. Sketch the mammal in the frame. Include a drawing of its track.

- ❏ Its size
- ❏ Its body covering
- ❏ Its food
- ❏ Its means of protecting itself
- ❏ Its habits

[sketch frame]

Write the mammal's English and Latin names:

_____

_____

Nature Noteboook: Draw and color a more detailed picture of the mammal and its track. Include its English and Latin names.

Copybook

Copy the second paragraph from this week's copybook selection into your copybook. Check your work, word by word, against the original.

Did you

☐ include every word in the original and spell every word correctly?
☐ capitalize every letter that is capitalized in the original?
☐ include every punctuation mark in the original?

Noun Review

From this week's copybook selection:

Write three proper nouns. Do they name persons, places, things, or ideas?

___

Write three common nouns that name things.

___

Write three common nouns that name ideas.

___

For each of the singular nouns below, write the plural form; for each of the plural nouns, write the singular form.

things   life   light

___

darkness   children   glory

___

Week 10 • Day 3

Today is _____
              Day   Date   Year

Read And Narrate

The Three Pigs
~ *Childhood's Favorites and Fairy Tales*, Edited by Mabie, Hale, and Forbush

Vocabulary to study before you read:

bundle	sternly	furze
politely	snug	trice
mortar	trowel	scampered
squire	butter-churn	blazing

Draw a picture or series of pictures illustrating the story.

Copybook

Copy the third paragraph and the attribution from this week's copybook selection into your copybook. Check your work, word by word, against the original.

Did you

❑ include every word in the original and spell every word correctly?
❑ capitalize every letter that is capitalized in the original?
❑ include every punctuation mark in the original?

Spelling Rule: I Before E

*Review the rule from Week 3. Look for words from this week's copybook selection with an ei or ie phonogram Write the **i before e** word from this week's copybook selection. Then write the **except after c** word. Notice that these two words rhyme.*

_____

Here are a few more exceptions you should memorize. Copy these.

sovereign   counterfeit   protein

_____

Noun & Pronoun Review

Write the alternate possessive form below, along with the thing possessed.

glory of Him   _____

lives of men   _____

children of God   _____

Creator of it   _____

truth of the gospels _____

Week 10 ~ Day 4

Today is _____
             Day   Date   Year

Picture Study _____

Week 10 • Day 4

Dictation

_____

_____

_____

_____

_____

_____

Homonyms, Synonyms, & Antonyms

Write one synonym and one antonym for each of these words.

dark _____

true _____

beginning _____

Write one or more homonyms for each of these words.

through _____

made _____

not _____

know _____

right _____

Drawing Page

from A Christmas Carol

Such a bustle ensued that you might have thought a goose the rarest of all birds; a feathered phenomenon, to which a black swan was a matter of course—and in truth it was something very like it in that house. Mrs. Cratchit made the gravy (ready beforehand in a little saucepan) hissing hot; Master Peter mashed the potatoes with incredible vigour; Miss Belinda sweetened up the apple-sauce; Martha dusted the hot plates; Bob took Tiny Tim beside him in a tiny corner at the table; the two young Cratchits set chairs for everybody, not forgetting themselves, and mounting guard upon their posts, crammed spoons into their mouths, lest they should shriek for goose before their turn came to be helped. At last the dishes were set on, and grace was said. It was succeeded by a breathless pause, as Mrs. Cratchit, looking slowly all along the carving-knife, prepared to plunge it in the breast; but when she did, and when the long expected gush of stuffing issued forth, one murmur of delight arose all round the board, and even Tiny Tim, excited by the two young Cratchits, beat on the table with the handle of his knife, and feebly cried Hurrah!

There never was such a goose. Bob said he didn't believe there ever was such a goose cooked. Its tenderness and flavour, size and cheapness, were the themes of universal admiration. Eked out by apple-sauce and mashed potatoes, it was a sufficient dinner for the whole family; indeed, as Mrs. Cratchit said with great delight (surveying one small atom of a bone upon the dish), they hadn't ate it all at last! Yet every one had had enough, and the youngest Cratchits in particular, were steeped in sage and onion to the eyebrows! But now, the plates being changed by Miss Belinda, Mrs. Cratchit left the room alone—too nervous to bear witnesses—to take the pudding up and bring it in.

~ Charles Dickens

Week 11 • Day 1

Today is _____
　　　　　　Day　　　　　　　Date　　　　　　Year

The Three Sillies
~ *Childhood's Favorites and Fairy Tales*, Edited by Mabie, Hale, and Forbush

Vocabulary to study before you read:

courted	draw	mallet
settle	aside	durst
coaxed	strangled	smothered
handkerchief	invented	shamefully

Draw a picture or series of pictures illustrating the story.

Week 11 • Day 1

Copybook

Copy the title and the first sentence of the first paragraph (it's long!) from this week's copybook selection into your copybook. Check your work, word by word, against the original.

Did you

☐ include every word in the original and spell every word correctly?

☐ capitalize every letter that is capitalized in the original?

☐ include every punctuation mark in the original?

Possessive Pronoun **Their** and Its Homonyms

A rule worth repeating: **Possessive pronouns NEVER use an apostrophe** *(Week 7). Here is a possessive pronoun which has homonyms. Learn to use these words correctly.*

- ✓ their   belonging to them
- ✓ they're   they + are (contraction)
- ✓ there   shows location or sometimes introduces a sentence

Rewrite the sentences below, substituting the correct word from the list above in place of the blank.

The Crachits delighted in ___ Christmas feast. ___ trying to keep from shrieking. The glorious goose is finally ___ on the table.

_____

_____

_____

_____

_____

Write an original sentence using the possessive pronoun their.

_____

_____

Week 11 • Day 2

Today is _____
　　　　　　Day　　　　　　　　Date　　　　　　　　　　　　Year

Nature Study

Choose a mammal, and talk about its characteristics, covering the points below. Sketch the mammal in the frame. Include a drawing of its track.

- ❑ Its size
- ❑ Its body covering
- ❑ Its food
- ❑ Its means of protecting itself
- ❑ Its habits

Write the mammal's English and Latin names:

_____

_____

Nature Noteboook: Draw and color a more detailed picture of the mammal and its track. Include its English and Latin names.

Week 11 • Day 2

Copybook

Copy the rest of the first paragraph and a sentence or two of the third from this week's copybook selection into your copybook. Check your work, word by word, against the original.

Did you

❑ include every word in the original and spell every word correctly?
❑ capitalize every letter that is capitalized in the original?
❑ include every punctuation mark in the original?

Noun Review

Write three proper nouns naming persons from this week's copybook selection, each of which has a title.

_____

_____

Review the rules for making nouns plural: For most words, add an **-s**. But if the ending of the word hisses, changes, or ends in **-o**, add **-es**. Find the plural word *potatoes* in this week's copybook selection. Copy it below, then write the singular form.

_____

_____

Write three other common plural nouns that name things.

_____

_____

For each of the singular nouns below, write the plural form; for each of the plural nouns, write the singular form.

    plates   knife   gush

    goose   bone   Cratchits

Week 11 • Day 3

Today is _____
                Day   Date   Year

Read And Narrate

Little Red Riding Hood
~ Childhood's Favorites and Fairy Tales, Edited by Mabie, Hale, and Forbush

Vocabulary to study before you read:

glades	thickets	thatched
latticed	dairy	brisk
copse	hollow	loitered
pattering	bobbin	hoarse
wheezed	bitterly	hearty

Draw a picture or series of pictures illustrating the story.

Copybook

Copy the third paragraph and the attribution from this week's copybook selection into your copybook. Check your work, word by word, against the original.

Did you

- ☐ include every word in the original and spell every word correctly?
- ☐ capitalize every letter that is capitalized in the original?
- ☐ include every punctuation mark in the original?

Noun & Pronoun Review

Rewrite the sentence below. For the underlined noun, substitute an appropriate pronoun. For the underlined pronoun, substitute the appropriate noun.

<u>It</u> was a sufficient dinner for <u>the family</u>.

_____

Write the alternate possessive form below, along with the thing possessed.

hiss of the gravy _____

flavour of the goose _____

tenderness of it _____

delight of Mrs. Cratchit _____

A very common spelling mistake is to write a plural noun using an apostrophe. This happens very often with proper names. Rewrite these sentences using the proper form of the name Cratchit (plural with no apostrophe or possessive with an apostrophe):

The ___ feast is approaching! The young ___ beat on the table.

_____

Week 11 • Day 4

Today is _____
　　　　　　　　Day　　　　　　　Date　　　　　　　Year

Picture Study

Dictation

_____
_____
_____
_____
_____
_____

Onomatopoeia

In this week's copybook selection, there are at least four examples of onomatopoeia. Write two of them below:

_____
_____

Homonyms, Synonyms, & Antonyms

Write:

a synonym for tiny   _____

an antonym for tiny   _____

a synonym for delight   _____

an antonym for delight   _____

a homonym for forth   _____

Drawing Page

from ONCE IN ROYAL DAVID'S CITY

Once in royal David's city
Stood a lowly cattle shed,
Where a mother laid her baby
In a manger for his bed:
Mary was that mother mild,
Jesus Christ her little child.

He came down to earth from Heaven,
Who is God and Lord of all,
And his shelter was a stable,
And his cradle was a stall;
With the poor, and mean, and lowly,
Lived on earth our Savior holy.

And our eyes at last shall see him,
Through his own redeeming love,
For that child so dear and gentle
Is our Lord in Heav'n above,
And He leads His children on
To the place where He is gone.

Not in that poor lowly stable,
With the oxen standing by,
We shall see him; but in Heaven,
Set at God's right hand on high;
Where like stars his children crowned
All in white shall wait around.

~ Cecil Frances Alexander

Week 12 • Day 1

Today is _____
                Day   Date   Year

Jack and the Beanstalk
~ *Childhood's Favorites and Fairy Tales*, Edited by Mabie, Hale, and Forbush

Vocabulary to study before you read:

bargain	halter	exchanging
beanstalk	gallant	slain
mistaken	bullock	lark
cackle	brandishing	strides

Draw a picture or series of pictures illustrating the story.

WEEK 12 • DAY 1

COPYBOOK

Copy the title and first stanza from this week's copybook selection into your copybook. Check your work, word by word, against the original.

Did you

☐ include every word in the original and spell every word correctly?
☐ capitalize every letter that is capitalized in the original?
☐ include every punctuation mark in the original?

RHYMING PAIRS

Each stanza of this hymn has a pair of rhyming words at the end of the second and fourth lines. Each stanza also has a pair of rhyming words at the end of the fifth and sixth lines.

From this week's copybook selection, write two rhyming pairs with endings that are spelled the same.

_____

_____

From this week's copybook selection, write three rhyming pairs with endings that are spelled differently.

_____

_____

*Write several words that rhyme with **dear**. At least one of them should have an ending that is spelled differently.*

_____

115

Week 12 ◆ Day 2

Today is _____
           Day   Date   Year

Nature Study

Choose a mammal, and talk about its characteristics, covering the points below. Sketch the mammal in the frame. Include a drawing of its track.

- ❑ Its size
- ❑ Its body covering
- ❑ Its food
- ❑ Its means of protecting itself
- ❑ Its habits

Write the mammal's English and Latin names:

_____

_____

Nature Noteboook: Draw and color a more detailed picture of the mammal and its track. Include its English and Latin names.

WEEK 12 • DAY 2

COPYBOOK

Copy the second and third stanzas from this week's copybook selection into your copybook. Check your work, word by word, against the original.

Did you

- ❏ include every word in the original and spell every word correctly?
- ❏ capitalize every letter that is capitalized in the original?
- ❏ include every punctuation mark in the original?

NOUN REVIEW

From this week's copybook selection, write three proper nouns naming persons.

_____

_____

Write three common nouns naming persons from this week's copybook selection.

_____

_____

Write three common nouns that name places from this week's copybook selection..

_____

_____

Write the plural forms of ox and cow from this week's copybook selection.

_____

_____

Write the alternate possessive form below, along with the thing possessed.

city of David   _____

right hand of God   _____

brightness of stars   _____

117

Week 12 • Day 3

Today is _____
              Day   Date   Year

Read And Narrate

Cinderella
~ Childhood's Favorites and Fairy Tales, Edited by Mabie, Hale, and Forbush

Vocabulary to study before you read:

noble	mockingly	frock
decking	cinders	transformed
liveries	wistfully	murmur
slyly	nonsense	particular
radiantly	herald	

Draw a picture or series of pictures illustrating the story.

Copybook

Copy the fourth stanza and the attribution from this week's copybook selection into your copybook. Check your work, word by word, against the original.

Did you

- ☐ include every word in the original and spell every word correctly?
- ☐ capitalize every letter that is capitalized in the original?
- ☐ include every punctuation mark in the original?

Possessive Pronouns **Your** & its Homonyms and **Whose** & its Homonyms

One more time: **Possessive pronouns NEVER use an apostrophe.** Here are two more possessive pronouns which have homonyms. Learn to use these words correctly.

- ✓ whose   belonging to whom
- ✓ who's   who + is (contraction)

Rewrite the sentences below, filling in the blank with the correct word, either whose or who's.

___ this baby ___ mother laid Him in a manger?

_____

_____

- ✓ your   belonging to you
- ✓ you're   you + are (contraction)

Rewrite the sentences below, filling in the blank with the correct word, either your or you're.

Jesus, ___ at the right hand of ___ Father.

_____

_____

Week 12 • Day 4

Today is _____
　　　　　　　　　　Day　　　　　　　　　　Date　　　　　　　　　　Year

Picture Study _____

_____

_____

_____

Week 12 • Day 4

Dictation

Homonyms, Synonyms, & Antonyms

Write:

a synonym for lowly _____

an antonym for royal _____

a synonym for shelter _____

an antonym for gentle _____

a homonym for eye _____

a homonym for where _____

Simile

Find the simile in this week's copybook selection. Remember that a simile must use the words like, as, or than. Write the two things being compared below.

_____ is compared to _____

Drawing Page

Drawing Page

Drawing Page

Drawing Page

Drawing Page

DRAWING PAGE

Drawing Page

Made in the USA
Columbia, SC
29 May 2019